Brief Couples Therapy:

Group and Individual Couple Treatment for Addiction and Related Mental Health Concerns

Gloria Chaim, MSW

Sharon Armstrong, PhD

Joanne Shenfeld, MSW

Colleen Kelly, MSW

Selina Li, MSW

Centre
for Addiction and
Mental Health
Centre de
toxicomanie et
de santé mentale

A Pan American Health Organization / World Health Organization Collaborating Centre

Brief Couples Therapy: Group and Individual Couple Treatment
for Addiction and Related Mental Health Concerns

National Library of Canada Cataloguing in Publication

Brief couples therapy : group and individual couple treatment for
addiction and related mental health concerns / Gloria Chaim ... [et al.].

Includes bibliographical references.
ISBN 0-88868-448-7

1. Substance abuse —Treatment. 2. Marital psychotherapy.
I. Chaim, Gloria, 1955– II. Centre for Addiction and Mental Health.

RC564.B748 2003   616.86'0651   C2003-901095-3

PG117

Printed in Canada
Copyright © 2003 Centre for Addiction and Mental Health

This book was produced by:
DEVELOPMENT
Caroline Hebblethwaite, CAMH
EDITORIAL
Diana Ballon, CAMH
Sue McCluskey, CAMH
DESIGN
Nancy Leung, CAMH
PRODUCTION
Christine Harris, CAMH
MARKETING
Ronda Kellington, CAMH

For information on other Centre for Addiction and Mental Health resource materials
or to place an order, please contact:
Marketing and Sales Services
Centre for Addiction and Mental Health
33 Russell Street
Toronto, ON M5S 2S1 Canada
Tel.: 1-800-661-1111 or 416-595-6059 in Toronto
E-mail: marketing@camh.net

Web site: www.camh.net

ACKNOWLEDGMENTS

EVALUATION TEAM
Selina Li
Virginia Ittig-Deland
Sharon Armstrong

PROJECT TEAM
Gloria Chaim
Joanne Shenfeld
Selina Li
Sharon Armstrong
Colleen Kelly
Carolynne Cooper
Tony Toneatto
Virginia Ittig-Deland
Dennis Walker

FIELD TEST SITES
Centre for Addiction and Mental Health,
    ARF Division, Family Service (CAMH)
Addiction Services for York Region (ASYR)
North York General Hospital, Branson Division,
    Mental Health Outpatient Services (NYGH)

FIELD TEST PARTNERS
Pam Santon, (ASYR)
David Ravvin, (ASYR)
Lisa Freud-Goldman, (NYGH)
Genevieve McNabb, (NYGH)

REVIEWERS
Charmaine C. Williams
Clare Bowles
Darryl Upfold
David Denberg
David Ravvin
Donna Akman
Elizabeth Hendren-Roberge
Elsbeth Tupker
Farzana Doctor
Genevieve McMath
Jane Paterson
John Mancini
Lisa Freud-Goldman
Pam Santon
Paul Stebbins
Sonia Panchyshyn
Wayne Skinner

We gratefully acknowledge the generous support
of the Stupp/Cohen Families Foundation and
their initiative to create the Randy Stupp Fellowship
at the Centre for Addiction and Mental Health.

CONTENTS

INTRODUCTION

Who Will Use This Manual?

This manual was developed primarily as a tool for therapists and counsellors working in substance use settings who would like to augment their practice by seeing couples. Clinicians intending to use this program should be familiar with solution-focused therapy, as well as couple and family therapy. Familiarity with cognitive behavioural interventions and communication theory would also be helpful.

The manual will also be useful for the practitioner who is seeing couples, and who would like to be able to offer a focused, specific program for clients presenting with substance use issues. In this situation, familiarity with cognitive behavioural therapy, relapse prevention and motivational interviewing for substance use is recommended.

CONCURRENT DISORDERS SETTINGS

Because the Brief Couples Therapy (BCT) protocol was developed and is used within a concurrent setting, we regard it as one aspect of a comprehensive approach to treatment for substance use and mental health disorders. As such, BCT focuses on substance use issues to a greater extent than on mental health issues. However, whether or not clients present themselves as suffering from concurrent disorders, therapists and counsellors will undoubtedly find themselves dealing with couples who have had to cope with depression, mania, anxiety and other mental health issues. Thus, therapists should be aware of the prevalence of concurrent disorders as described in this manual in the section "Why is there a need for Brief Multiple Couple Treatment?" In particular, therapists should be cognizant of the likelihood that clients may engage in their substance use or increase it when they are dealing with mental health problems such as depression, anxiety, schizophrenia and personality disorders; and on the other side of the coin, therapists ought to be aware of the possibility of the occurrence of symptoms of anxiety, depression and psychotic episodes that are tied to problem substance use.

THEORETICAL AND PHILOSOPHICAL PERSPECTIVES

It is hoped that this manual will be a useful tool for clinicians who may adhere to a variety of different philosophical and theoretical perspectives on human nature and change processes. Because the underlying conceptual model is based on an integration of theoretical principles, we believe that the techniques we are presenting are adaptable to different schools of thought. In this vein, we hope that whatever your philosophy of human nature or your theoretical perspective regarding the processes involved in counselling and therapy, you will find this a useful tool for practice. We presume that, where deemed necessary, therapists will modify the wording of checklists and exercises to suit their particular clientele, practices and philosophies.

Who Is BCT For?

The clients who have engaged in the BCT treatment program, in both the individual and the group conditions, have come from a variety of backgrounds, but all of them have had problems with substance use and many have had concurrent mental health issues. Prior to being in couples treatment, the person with the substance use problem has had treatment or has met his or her personal drug-use goal, or both. This has enabled the work of the sessions to be focused on the relationship issues connected to substance use to a greater extent than on the individual client's use. Therefore, we recommend that therapists using BCT ensure either that the substance-using partner has met his or her personal substance goal and has received individual treatment or that the client is currently receiving treatment for substance use. Nevertheless, lapses during the course of this treatment, or any, may occur, and these should be dealt with during sessions in the context of their impact on partners' relationships.

BCT is designed to assist couples who have made a commitment to remaining in their relationship and who have demonstrated a willingness to work on the issues that brought them into counselling. For example, a couple may enter therapy in order to re-establish trust that has been lost due to substance use, and it can then be important for each partner to be prepared to explore the ways in which trust has been altered as he or she begins to look at moving forward as a couple.

Contraindications include threats of violence; instability with regard to mental health issues, such as being suicidal or having active psychoses; and couples who are not invested in working through issues. Each of these contraindications should be assessed during the initial assessment interview, and with respect either to the threat of violence or acute mental health problems, referrals should be made to appropriate services. It is expected that clients with current mental health issues have reached a level of stability that would allow them to participate in a couples group treatment, and that they would be connected to a primary therapist for any ongoing mental health problems, such as depression, mania, anxiety or personality disorders.

When one or both partners are not committed to working towards change in the relationship, this therapy protocol may be inappropriate for them, particularly the group format — for example, when one partner refuses to stop or decrease his or her substance use so that work can be done on relationship issues. Some elements, like the Miracle Question, may help couples clarify commitment issues and decide whether or not they want to work together towards positive change; yet if it seems likely that a couple's objective is to separate, that goal would sidetrack the group process. In that case, counselling would be best managed through individual couple sessions. If a couple are undecided as to their commitment to making changes in their relationship, we would suggest that they could participate in the group if they met the following criterion: they would need to be prepared to commit to working together for the duration of the sessions to explore whether or not change were possible.

Why Is There a Need for Brief Couples Treatment?

Brief Couples Therapy (BCT) is an eight-session, structured treatment for couples with substance abuse and related mental health concerns that can be delivered in either individual couple format with one therapist, or in a group format — of up to four couples — with two therapists. Over the course of eight weeks, couples learn to identify and reduce problems stemming from substance use, including problematic family interaction patterns, and communication styles. They will begin to establish concrete, attainable goals, build trust and intimacy, and establish relapse prevention strategies.

COUPLE INVOLVEMENT

In both the areas of substance use and mental health treatment, there is a substantial literature supporting various types of family involvement and intervention as the main mode of intervention or as an adjunct to it (Stanton & Heath, 1997; Baucom et al., 1998). Health Canada's *Best Practices: Substance Abuse Treatment and Rehabilitation* (1999) supports the effectiveness of marital behavioural therapy as well as group treatments. The effectiveness of couple involvement in the treatment of problem substance use has been widely documented in the past two decades (Kaufman, 1985; Zweben et al., 1988; Montag & Wilson, 1992; Shadish et al., 1993; Edwards & Steinglass, 1995; Pinsof & Wynne, 1995; Fals-Stewart et al., 1996; Stanton & Shadish, 1997; Epstein & McCrady, 1998; O'Farrell & Feehan, 1999; O'Farrell & Fals-Stewart, 2000). This research has shown that spousal involvement in treatment is effective in motivating people with alcohol problems to enter and continue treatment. Moreover, it has shown that different models of couple therapy have produced significant reduction in alcohol or drug use and improvement in marital functioning. However, despite the growing evidence that spousal involvement in treatment increases treatment retention and improves outcomes, addiction treatment continues to be focused on the substance-using individual in most settings.

As treatment resources become increasingly scarce and waiting lists grow, it is crucial to develop effective treatment interventions from both outcome and cost perspectives. It is also important to note that the majority of the treatment literature does not address issues related to cultural and sexual diversity. In order to address these gaps, CAMH is utilizing a number of brief treatment approaches for a diverse clientele, and the treatment protocol presented in this manual is one of a number of these brief treatment approaches.

GROUP FORMAT

Treatment groups have a long history and are widely used in the addiction field, as they have been shown to result in decreased costs as well as improved outcomes (Roberts et al., 1999). In early studies of couples group therapy for alcoholism, couples groups were introduced mainly as an adjunct to inpatient programs. These studies provided some evidence for the efficacy of couples group treatment for alcohol problems. Today, the emerging research evaluating couples group therapy for outpatient treatment of alcohol problems suggests positive outcomes for couples treatment in the group format (Corder et al., 1972; Cadogan, 1973; McCrady et al., 1979; Hahlweg et al., 1982; Bowers & Al-Redha, 1990; Baucom et al., 1998; O'Farrell et al., 1998; O'Farrell & Fals-Stewart, 2000).

In view of the foregoing, some of the potential benefits of multiple couples therapy for addictions are: decreasing waiting lists; reducing treatment costs and increasing treatment retention; improving treatment outcomes (i.e., achieving substance use goals and improving couple satisfaction); providing a forum for demonstrating communication and problem-solving strategies; providing feedback and positive reinforcement from peers, which may also improve treatment retention and outcomes; modelling positive coping styles; and decreasing highly dysfunctional behaviours.

CONCURRENT DISORDERS

Estimates of lifetime drug-use disorders comorbid with alcohol dependence are as high as 80 per cent (Epstein & McCrady, 1998). Here at CAMH, over 50 per cent of clients presenting for treatment in the Addiction Programs reported drugs other than alcohol as their primary problem substance, and about 40 per cent reported more than one problem substance. About 50 per cent of these clients also screened positive on the Psychiatric Screener (a screening tool in development at CAMH) for mental disorders such as schizophrenia, mood, anxiety and eating disorders. Correspondingly high rates of comorbidity have also been published by large-scale studies in the United States.[1]

In addition, as the general and treatment populations become more diverse, it is important that treatment protocols and approaches address the severity and complexity of presenting problems, learning styles and ethno/sexual/racial/cultural dimensions. Where suitable, group interventions are preferable

---

[1] See Daley & Moss (Chapter 1; 2002) for prevalence rates of dual disorders in the United States.

for the cost-benefit reasons outlined above. However, options for individual couple interventions and other individual and family interventions need to be available as well.

For 20 years, the members of our team of experienced clinicians have been offering couple treatment in the conjoint format for clients who present with substance use problems; and for the past five years, we have offered this treatment for clients with concurrent disorders. Drawing upon the clinicians' experience, a BCT treatment program incorporating cognitive, behavioural and systems approaches is presently being researched and delivered. It is believed that this program will contribute to more efficient service delivery, lower treatment attrition rates and better treatment outcomes. We are hopeful that research utilizing the BCT model of therapy outlined in this manual will generate a broader conceptualization of the needs of couples and families with substance use and mental health issues and that, in turn, further refinement and extension of the treatment model will produce interventions that are germane to wider family constellations and to broader ethno/sexual/racial/cultural communities.

Development of the Manual

An early draft of the manual was piloted in a research project at CAMH. Following further refinement, the manual was distributed to clinicians at CAMH, as well as to therapists and counsellors from external agencies, to test its usefulness with individual couples and multiple couple groups. A more complete draft of the manual was reviewed by 19 different consultants, clinicians and researchers practising in the areas of mental health, addictions, general family services and private practice. As a result of these reviews, the manual was further refined and adapted to become a useful tool for clinicians working with couples with addictions and mental health concerns. Currently, the manual is being utilized within a multi-site research project comparing group versus individual couple therapy with a diverse sample of couple clients.

The treatment model has been field tested at CAMH, North York General Hospital and Addiction Services For York Region (ASYR). A six-month outcome evaluation of the model is under way. Preliminary results show that the program (in both group and individual formats) has been well received by the clients. From the field test, we have also obtained qualitative data from the clinicians in the form of comments about the usefulness of the manual, its readability and flow. As well, over 30 post-session problem-solving debriefing meetings have been conducted with clinicians who are administering the treatment. Feedback from these sessions has been incorporated into the development of this manual.

The Integrative Model[2]

BCT is based on the Integrative Model of family/couple treatment that grew from scrutiny of our own practice in a family treatment team at the former Addiction Research Foundation, now the Centre for Addiction and Mental Health (CAMH), where we work with a diverse population. Over the years, the severity of presenting problems, and the frequency of comorbidity of substance use and mental health concerns, have increased tremendously. As a result, we have adapted our model to working with clients with concurrent disorders. The Integrative Model is seen as an effective way of intervening on multi-dimensional levels, an important consideration when working with concurrently disordered clients and their families.

---

[2] See Appendix A for "The Background of the Integrative Model."

Substance use and mental health are the presenting focus of family concern and the main targets of intervention. At its core, the Integrative Model is an assimilation of theoretical assumptions and techniques from the family therapies, solution-focused therapy and cognitive behaviour therapy that were deemed relevant to the treatment of families and couples faced with substance use issues. The hallmarks of the treatment approaches that the model draws upon are as follows:

- observing cross-generational patterns of family interactions and their effects on present relationships (intergenerational)
- attending to boundaries and coalitions (structural)
- tracking and attempting to change key patterns of interaction (strategic)
- focusing on strengths, making small changes and creating solutions (solution-focused)
- using self-monitoring and focusing on identifying and addressing cognitions and overt, observable behaviour (cognitive behavioural).

Each perspective provides a unique orientation, and taken as an integrated whole, the Integrative Model of therapy allows the clinician to fully address all the issues of concern; something that could not be accomplished as efficiently by any of the treatment modalities alone. The Integrative Model is flexible, making it applicable to families at all stages of clinical contact, from intake to termination, to families at various stages of the life cycle and to different family configurations (multicultural, blended, single-parent, etc.). New approaches and techniques can be incorporated into the model because it is non-prescriptive, and provides the therapist with a number of intervention options rather than limiting the therapist to a particular technique to be used in specific circumstances. The interplay of clinician preference, agency factors, and client needs and strengths will influence the application of the model. This model has been developed specifically for use with families experiencing problems related to concurrent disorders, and is well suited to the range and depth of difficulties that can be present in these situations.

Brief Couples Therapy (BCT)

By incorporating the theory and techniques from the Integrative Model, BCT is a powerful tool for couples with substance use problems.

Often, couple and family therapists find themselves in the position of being referees for family or couple "boxing matches," when family members have become entrenched within their own positions and are unable to see the problem from each other's point of view. Alcohol and drug use can exacerbate this type of blaming and positioning. Thus, the family systems perspective allows therapists to get a broader scope in relation to reoccurring issues.

Therapists can use this broader awareness to help each member of the couple gain an understanding of the frames of reference underlying the rigid positions that each has taken in his or her ongoing conflicts. When the family systems framework is combined with solution-focused aims, such as looking towards a more positive future and increasing self-efficacy, couples can begin to resolve complex substance-related problems by looking at these problems from a different perspective and imagining possibilities for change.

Finally, principles that were derived from the social learning and cognitive behavioural modalities and that inform the Integrative Model provide the substance that underlies skill-building strategies. These strategies, we believe, help couples to increase positive communication and to enhance their relationship between sessions.

Tips on Implementing the Program

DIFFERENCES BETWEEN GROUP AND INDIVIDUAL COUPLE SESSIONS

An important difference between individual and group sessions is the time allocated to each couple. There is more time available when working with an individual couple. This allows the therapist to clarify issues, work on a specific goal, explore in more depth differences and meanings, and highlight positive changes that may be occurring during the therapy sessions.

Individual couples do not experience feedback from other group members — a process found to be extremely valuable for couples in the group session. In the individual sessions, the extra time for in-depth exploration of issues may make up for this discrepancy.

The total number of sessions for clients in the group situation is nine (one assessment and eight treatment sessions), while the total number of sessions for clients in the individual situation is eight, because the assessment session and the first session are combined for individual couples.

The process of checking in and checking out can be simplified for individual couples by just asking the couple to identify how they are feeling at that moment.

The difference in materials for conducting individual sessions versus group sessions is minimal. For either type, therapists should review the checklists for each session. The checklists are written from the group position. Instructions that are more suited to conducting a group session may be ignored for the individual session. Following each session checklist and summary, there is also a Tips for Individual Couple Session sheet, which highlights any notable variation between the individual versus the group format.

Sessions should be scheduled on a weekly basis. Individual sessions, however, may be on a more varying timetable than group sessions. When there is a long gap between sessions, therapists should ask if anything has changed.

GENERAL TIPS AND COUNSELLING ISSUES

The following are general recommendations about how to deal with some of the issues that may occur during Brief Couples Therapy (BCT). These recommendations are suggestions only, to be followed at the discretion of the user. When dealing with specific problems or crises, we expect that you will be guided by the ethical mandates of your profession and the procedures of the agency within which you work.

Check-in

When asking clients about "issues arising from the last session," therapists should use their judgment about allowing as much time for this exploration as is needed without getting sidetracked from the aim of the session. Any lingering or ongoing issues that emerge should be woven into the content and process of the group as outlined in the protocol for that session.

Homework

1. For clients who have trouble with the reading level of the homework or with writing, or for those clients whose first language is not English, therapists may wish to adapt or translate the homework exercises to fit the needs of their clients. We have discovered that partners sometimes help each other

with the homework. Although we generally encourage partners to do their homework assignments individually, occasionally it may be practical for partners to help each other, particularly with the clarification of instructions.

2. Although not encouraged, if someone has forgotten to do his or her homework in between sessions, the homework can be done during the session.

3. Couples should keep their homework between sessions. Often the homework from one session flows naturally into the homework for the next session, and it can be helpful for couples to refer back to previous session homework.

Time Management

Therapists should try to ensure that each couple is allotted equal session time. Occasionally, this is not possible. When one or more couples do not have the opportunity to fully share their homework or to discuss issues, therapists should utilize material from the couple who are currently sharing in order to advance the educational experience of that session. (e.g., because some couples find it difficult to grasp the point of the Miracle Question as an exercise in self-exploration of needs, goals and change, it can be useful for therapists to spend a greater amount of time exploring one couple's miracle in the session to provide an example for others to practise outside of that session).

Missed Sessions

Couples should be informed as to the importance of making a commitment to attend the entire eight sessions, both for their own benefit and for the overall functioning of the group. When a couple have to miss a session, they should give as much notice as possible. Therapists may then wish to give homework instructions by phone. If more than one couple have to miss the same session, the therapists may decide to postpone that session. Occasionally, one partner may have to come to a session alone. That can be preferable to having both partners miss the session. However, therapists should clarify that the couples are expected to show up together and, when deemed necessary, the other partner should be contacted by phone to clarify her or his commitment. In the individual therapy sessions, if one partner shows up alone, the therapist should reschedule the individual couple session.

Management of Mental Health Crises

If a client should come to a session in a state of acute mental illness (e.g., suicidal, threatening or psychotic), appropriate contact should be made with the nearest emergency room or primary practitioner.

Management of Relationship Crises

Relationship crises may be related to ongoing mental health or substance use concerns. If the issue appears to be related to medication management, then the client should be referred to his or her primary medical practitioner. Some couples may come into sessions with occasional or recurrent relationship crises. In that case, focusing on session tasks can be an effective way to reduce the emotional intensity that deters couples from dealing with therapeutic issues. Communication skills are introduced in Session 5. Prior to that session, if ineffective communication skills seem to be impairing couples' ability to work on their relationship, the Tips for Effective Communication sheet (page 64) can be handed out, and a brief discussion can take place about practising effective communication skills between sessions. Couples should be reminded that there will be specific session time devoted to working on communication skills in upcoming sessions as well.

Substance Use

If a client shows up under the influence of drugs or alcohol, therapists may need to remind the client that he or she is required to show up sober and to ask the individual to leave that session. In such a case, the client should be contacted prior to the next session to re-establish the therapeutic alliance and the client's commitment to the therapy. The focus of this treatment is the couple's relationship rather than substance use; however, depending on the requirements of the agency, therapists may wish to ask about substance use during check-in and to keep track of it in the session progress note. Exploration regarding the impact of the reported substance use on the relationship should be incorporated into the session tasks, as opposed to becoming a separate focus.

Taping

Taping sessions, with appropriate consent, can be useful for peer review and team training. If you intend to videotape or audiotape sessions, always check your equipment prior to starting the session. Tapes should be kept in a locked cabinet and clients should be made aware of the duration of time tapes will be kept, as well as how and when tapes will be destroyed.

How to Use the Manual

The clinical materials used in Brief Couples Therapy (BCT) consist of four types:
1. Session Guidelines
   Objectives
   Checklists
2. Session Resources
   Materials
   Summaries
   Tips
3. Handouts (marked with H under page number)
4. Progress Notes.

The session checklists are to be used by counsellors. These checklists outline the key topics to be covered in each session. The summaries that follow each checklist provide a handy outline that can be used for in-session reference. Session checklists give the order in which in-session exercises are usually completed, and they include examples of how to introduce, explain and utilize each of the exercises. Therapists should read the appropriate checklist before each session. Note that the size of the checklist-item descriptions is not necessarily associated with the amount of time required for the in-session components. For example, the check-in description is quite short, but the actual time taken to check in can vary considerably, depending on the size and needs of the group. Therapists should plan ahead to ensure that adequate time is allotted for each component of the session. Comments, tips and clinical interpretations from therapists who have used the materials and contributed to the project are also included to facilitate use of the materials. Therapists should familiarize themselves with all of the sessions in this manual prior to the first therapy session, so that they can re-order the sessions to match the needs of the group or the couple as necessary.

The handouts included after each of the session checklist summaries provide clinical exercises and materials that are to be used by clients. Most handouts are given to clients at the end of each session. It is intended that they be completed as homework for the following session. The homework assignments will become the focus of each session, so it is important that therapists emphasize the need for homework completion.

The progress notes list the key topics that are covered in each session. These notes provide an opportunity for reporting on client substance use and goal achievement. Additional space is also provided for other issues that are specific to the particular client. The progress notes are designed to be efficient and easy to use, while capturing pertinent clinical information.

With respect to the materials, the differences between individual and group sessions are minimal. For either type of session, therapists should review the checklists prior to each session. The checklists are written from the perspective of running a group. Tips for conducting an individual couple session follow each checklist and summary.

ASSESSMENT SESSION

Due to copyright restrictions, pages 9 and 10

• Dyadic Adjustment Scale (Sample Items)

have been deleted from this PDF file.

ASSESSMENT SESSION

Session Guidelines

CHECKLIST

Guidelines for the Counsellor	Tips on What to Do with or Say to the Client
1. Describing the purpose of brief couples therapy (BCT)	"People have different ideas about what treatment is about. Let me tell you something about this program. This program is for couples who are willing to look at how alcohol and/or drug use affect their lives. It helps couples improve their relationship by working on communication, problem solving, conflict reduction and other identified issues. It helps couples work on their drug use goals and ways to deal with relapse. It is based on the belief that your partner can help in your effort to change your alcohol/drug use."
2. Describing how BCT works	"This program is really to help you look at the impact of your substance use on your relationship and how your partner can help support you in your effort to change your drug use. To help with that, the program will involve eight sessions, which will begin following an assessment appointment with a therapist. Topics covered in these sessions will include family history, communication, trust, goal setting, problem solving and relapse prevention. Please attend the sessions with your partner and arrive alcohol- and drug-free."
3. Describing Who Comes to BCT	(This is especially important when providing BCT in a group format.) "You might also be wondering what the people who come into this program are like. While everybody has their own unique situation, here are some of the things we know about the people who come here . . ." (Give a general description of the clients seeking treatment at your agency.)
4. Completing the Client Background Information Form	This form can be completed as the couple is interviewed for assessment information.

5. Administering Standard Questionnaires	Ask both clients to complete 2 forms: the Alcohol and Drug Use Information Form and the Dyadic Adjustment Scale (optional). If the DAS is used, we recommend that you administer it before the Alcohol and Drug Use Information Form, so that you can score it while the clients are completing the latter form.
6. Feedback	Summarize and interpret scores from the forms that are used. Based on the overall assessment interview, go over main issues for the couple and tie this feedback to the treatment plan.
7. Preparation for the Next Appointment	If group: do a general orientation for the group and give them the start date. If individual: set the next appointment and hand out homework for Assignment 1 (Genogram/Family Tree). Discuss any barriers to attending treatment.

Session Resources

ASSESSMENT QUESTIONNAIRES: DESCRIPTION

Client Background Information Form

This form records the background information of both partners. The therapist can fill this in as the couple are interviewed. This provides a structure for obtaining pertinent information that will be useful for assessing the eligibility of the couple for BCT and for the formulation of a treatment plan.

Dyadic Adjustment Scale (DAS)

The DAS is a 32-item self-administered measure of the quality of marriage and similar dyads. It can be completed in about 10 minutes and has been widely used in research on the marital or dyadic relationship. Content, criterion-related and construct validity were reported; and the scale was found to have an overall reliability of .96 using Cronbach's coefficient alpha (Spanier, 1976; Spanier & Thompson, 1982). The DAS score is computed by adding up the scores of all items. Total score ranges from 0 to 151. There is no norm for determining the cut-off for happy or unhappy relationship. However, in a previous study, the mean score of a divorced sample is 71, and the mean score of a married sample is 115. A score below 71 may be indicative of a "distressed" relationship, and a score above 115 may be indicative of a "non-distressed" relationship.

It is not necessary for therapists to use this scale in their assessments for BCT. The authors used it in conjunction with the associated research study. However, we also found it helpful as a clinical tool. Clinically, the scale can be used in three ways:
- as a very general indicator, to help formulate an overall impression of the quality of the relationship
- to compare partners' responses, and then use the similarities and differences as a starting point for discussion
- to identify specific problem areas by examining responses to individual items, and to use these responses as a basis for discussion and the development of a treatment plan.

The DAS can be purchased from Multi-Health Systems.

Alcohol and Drug Use Information Form

This is a simplified version of the Drug Use History Questionnaire and Adverse Consequences of Drug Use Scale contained in the standardized assessment package for assessing substance use at the Centre for Addiction and Mental Health. This provides an evaluation of the substance use problem in terms of frequency of drug use, as well as its adverse consequences.

CLIENT BACKGROUND INFORMATION FORM

Client Name: _____	Client Name: _____
File No.: _____	File No.: _____
Date of Birth |__|__|__|__|__|__| DAY MONTH YEAR	Date of Birth |__|__|__|__|__|__| DAY MONTH YEAR
Sex ☐ Male ☐ Female ☐ TG/TS	Sex ☐ Male ☐ Female ☐ TG/TS
Education (years completed) |__|__|	Education (years completed) |__|__|
Occupation _____	Occupation _____

Current Employment Status	Current Employment Status
☐ Full-time employment	☐ Full-time employment
☐ Part-time employment	☐ Part-time employment
☐ Self-employed	☐ Self-employed
☐ Unemployed	☐ Unemployed
☐ Homemaker	☐ Homemaker
☐ Student	☐ Student

Currently living with *(check all that apply)*

☐ Spouse/partner
☐ Children
☐ Parents
☐ Other relatives/friends
☐ Alone

Currently living with *(check all that apply)*

☐ Spouse/partner
☐ Children
☐ Parents
☐ Other relatives/friends
☐ Alone

Number of past long-term
relationships/marriages   \|__\|__\|

Number of past long-term
relationships/marriages   \|__\|__\|

Length of marriage/
living together   \|__\|__\| MONTHS
OR
\|__\|__\| YEARS

Number of children (from
current/past relationships)
living with couple   \|__\|__\|

Number of separations
in this union   \|__\|__\|

Primary Substance of Abuse
(the one substance about which client is most concerned)
☐ No drug use problem

Check only one
☐ Alcohol problem
☐ Cocaine problem
☐ Heroin problem
☐ Marijuana (Cannabis) problem
☐ Tobacco problem
☐ Other drug(s) _____

Problem duration ⊔⊔⊔ MONTHS
OR
⊔⊔⊔ YEARS

Other Substance of Abuse
(any other substances for which client has some concerns)
Check all that apply
☐ Alcohol problem
☐ Cocaine problem
☐ Heroin problem
☐ Marijuana (Cannabis) problem
☐ Tobacco problem
☐ Other drug, specify: _____

Currently receiving treatment for substance use
(including AA or similar self-help groups)?
☐ Yes
☐ No
If YES, describe _____

Currently receiving treatment for emotional/
psychological difficulties?
☐ Yes
☐ No
If YES, describe _____

Previous Treatment for Alcohol/Drug Problem:
Check all that apply
☐ Detox
☐ Emergency
☐ Outpatient
☐ Inpatient
☐ Others: _____

Primary Substance of Abuse
(the one substance about which client is most concerned)
☐ No drug use problem

Check only one
☐ Alcohol problem
☐ Cocaine problem
☐ Heroin problem
☐ Marijuana (Cannabis) problem
☐ Tobacco problem
☐ Other drug(s) _____

Problem duration ⊔⊔⊔ MONTHS
OR
⊔⊔⊔ YEARS

Other Substance of Abuse
(any other substances for which client has some concerns)
Check all that apply
☐ Alcohol problem
☐ Cocaine problem
☐ Heroin problem
☐ Marijuana (Cannabis) problem
☐ Tobacco problem
☐ Other drug, specify: _____

Currently receiving treatment for substance use
(including AA or similar self-help groups)?
☐ Yes
☐ No
If YES, describe: _____

Currently receiving treatment for emotional/
psychological difficulties?
☐ Yes
☐ No
If YES, describe _____

Previous Treatment for Alcohol/Drug Problem:
Check all that apply
☐ Detox
☐ Emergency
☐ Outpatient
☐ Inpatient
☐ Others: _____

Commitment to Working on Relationship Issues:

_____

_____

_____

Treatment Goals:

_____

_____

_____

Domestic Violence Issues (past or present):

_____

_____

_____

Mental Health Issues:

_____

_____

_____

Other information (Previous couple therapy; Legal issues, etc):

_____

_____

_____

This page blocked for copyright reasons

ALCOHOL AND DRUG USE INFORMATION FORM

Name: _____　　Date: _____

Please answer the following questions about your alcohol and drug use:

Drug Type	Used in past 12 months?		No. of days used in past 90 days	Has your use of this substance been a concern to you?	
	Yes	No		Yes	No
ALCOHOL	☐	☐		☐	☐
CANNABIS pot, grass, hash	☐	☐		☐	☐
COCAINE/CRACK	☐	☐		☐	☐
BENZODIAZEPINES tranquillizers, Librium®, Valium®	☐	☐		☐	☐
PRESCRIPTION OPIOIDS methadone, painkillers, Percodan®, Darvon®, 292s®, Dilaudid®	☐	☐		☐	☐
OVER-THE-COUNTER CODEINE PREPARATIONS 222s®, Benylin®	☐	☐		☐	☐
HEROIN/OPIUM	☐	☐		☐	☐
HALLUCINOGENS acid, LSD, mushrooms, ecstasy	☐	☐		☐	☐
OTHER PSYCHOACTIVE DRUGS e.g. antidepressants, anti-alcohol drugs Specify names:					
(1) _____	☐	☐		☐	☐
(2) _____	☐	☐		☐	☐
(3) _____	☐	☐		☐	☐

As a result of your substance use, have you experienced the following problems in the past 90 days?

	Yes	No	N/A
Problems with your health	☐	☐	
Blackouts or memory problems, forgetting, confusion, difficulty thinking	☐	☐	
Mood changes, personality changes, substance-related problems, flashbacks when using	☐	☐	
Problems in relationships	☐	☐	
Being verbally or physically abusive when using	☐	☐	
Work or school problems	☐	☐	☐ (NO JOB OR NOT IN SCHOOL)
Legal problems (substance-related charges)	☐	☐	
Financial problems	☐	☐	
Has your partner's alcohol and/or drug use been a concern to you?	☐	☐	

If yes, please specify:

_____

_____

_____

_____

_____

FACTS ABOUT COUPLES TREATMENT

What is the program about?

Brief Couples Treatment:

- is for couples who are willing to look at how alcohol and/or drug use and/or addictive behaviours affect their lives
- helps couples improve their relationship by working on communication, problem solving, conflict reduction and other identified issues
- helps couples work on their drug use goals and ways to deal with relapse
- is based on the beliefs that substance use affects your relationship, that change in substance use affects your relationship, and that changes in your relationship can have an effect on alcohol or other drug use.

How does it work?

- The program will involve eight sessions, which will begin following an assessment appointment with a therapist.
- Topics covered in these sessions will include family history, communication, trust, goal setting, problem solving and relapse prevention.
- Please attend the sessions with your partner and arrive alcohol- and drug-free.

You have an appointment with _____

on _____   at _____

If for any reason you cannot keep your appointment, please call.

INTRODUCTION

Session Guidelines

Session Resources

Client Handouts

Session Guidelines

OBJECTIVES

Couples will:

- understand the purpose, format and content of the Brief Couples Therapy (BCT) treatment
- introduce themselves and begin to engage with the group
- identify some preliminary short- and long-term goals and expectations.

A safe, comfortable environment will be created through building group cohesion and reinforcing common issues among participants.

CHECKLIST

Guidelines for the Counsellor	Tips on What to Do with or Say to the Client
1. Therapists Introduce Themselves to the Group	Therapists will introduce themselves and describe their role. This can be a general introduction about who they are, their responsibilities and their role in helping to facilitate the group.
2. Reviewing Participation in the Group— Group Norms and Confidentiality	Safety: "This group is a place where you can start talking about and hopefully solving some of the problems you're facing in your relationship. Because people are going to be sharing things, it is important that we all agree that what is said in the group stays in the group. As you feel comfortable with us and with each other, you may be sharing personal information, and we want to make it safe for everyone to talk about your issues."
	Confidentiality: "Something that is important for us to talk about is confidentiality. What is said in here stays in this room. We need your permission to talk to or to release information to others outside of the family treatment team. However, there are some limits to confidentiality. If you are going to harm yourself or others, or if there are concerns about a child being at risk for harm, or when records are subpoenaed by the courts, then legally we need to break confidentiality. But aside from those exceptions, your confidentiality is maintained."
	Contact between Sessions: "This city can be a small place, and we're asking you please not to have contact with other group members outside the group while the sessions are in progress."

Respectful Communication: "A group expectation is that we all communicate in a respectful manner (i.e., no put-downs)."

Timekeeper: "An important part of doing any group is trying to keep everyone focused and to keep us all on track. So we will be watching the clock and may have to interject from time to time."

3. Client Introductions

Introductions Using an Icebreaker: "In today's session, we are going to be talking a lot and getting to know one another better. As a way of starting this, we would like you to [introduce icebreaker]."

Icebreaker Example: "Think about the situation in which you first met and identify a funny or happy memory of that time."

4. Stating the Format and the Rules of the Group

Attendance: "This group will be meeting for about an hour and a half once a week for eight weeks. Please attend all sessions with your partner and arrive alcohol- and drug-free. We'll start at ___ p.m. Because the functioning of the group as a whole relies on input from each of the members, it is important that you commit to coming to every group and that you arrive on time."

Format: "The framework for today's group will be similar to each of the remaining sessions. All of you will have the opportunity to talk about yourselves and your families in turn. Each week, we will use a different exercise to help you with communication, problem solving, goal setting and other relationship-building and relapse-prevention skills."

Roles: "This is your group and you are here to help each other out. Therefore what you have to say to each other is very important. We (the therapists) are here to help provide a safe environment and to encourage you to participate."

5. Stating the Purpose of the Treatment Group

"The purpose of the group is to help couples with substance use concerns to address the impact that their substance use has had on their relationship and to identify goals for change. It is also to help you focus on the present, and to have you think about how you would like your relationship to be in the future. An additional purpose of the group is to provide a supportive context where participants can benefit from others' experience and feedback. Aspects of supportive feedback are listening carefully, taking a non-judgmental position and responding in a clear, brief, specific manner, from an 'I' position."

Hand out the Description of Topics sheet or show a flipchart of the topics that will be covered in the eight sessions.

6. Exploring Clients' Expectations and Concerns	Ask all of the participants to state in turn their hopes and expectations for themselves as a couple during this group and to briefly describe their drug use history, treatment history and drug use goals. Therapists should encourage clients to focus on couple-related goals.
7. Homework (Genogram/Family Tree)	When handing out folders, instruct participants to keep all homework in their folders and bring them each week.

The symbols used in the Family Tree exercise may be changed to suit the needs of different agencies or clientele. (For example, we use circles to denote females and squares to denote males; these symbols may not be useful for transgendered or transsexual clients). Similarly, the sample Family Tree is only one example of a possible family tree that might be used.

NOTE
Therapists who have not done a genogram/family tree before should do one of their own to gain a better understanding of the exercise.

Describe the genogram as a "family tree," and explain its purpose: "We are going to do a type of family tree that can be helpful for understanding family background and different patterns or issues that may be important in your current relationship, but that date back to your family of origin. Please use this sample to help you to complete a family tree for your family, going back to your parents or grandparents if you feel this is important."

Demonstrate the use of a family tree: Prior to the group, therapists will have copied some or all of the Family Tree example, or a different example that they made up, onto a flipchart sheet (width-wise if possible). Put up the flipchart example, describe the different components of the chart and explain the linkages. "We will share your family trees with the group next week, as a way of getting to know each other better and putting your current relationship into a broader context. Please only include information you are comfortable sharing with the group; you may have other information you want to share later with your spouse."

Hand out folder packages: "This will be your folder for you to keep your homework and refer to from week to week. Inside you will find the Family Tree instruction sheets and a blank flipchart page for your family tree."

8. Check-out

Ask each group member to offer one word, thought or feeling as a check-out for the evening. The therapist may begin with "I feel hopeful" and go around the room.

Session Resources

MATERIALS
- one package per person, including one folder, the Family Tree example, instruction sheet, blank self-adhesive flipchart page
- Family Tree example on a flipchart sheet
- flipchart, markers
- liquid refreshments

SUMMARY

1. Therapists Introduce Themselves to the Group

2. Reviewing Participation in the Group — Group Norms and Confidentiality
   Safety
   Confidentiality
   Contact between Sessions
   Respectful Communication
   Timekeeper

3. Client Introductions
   Icebreaker

4. Stating the Format and the Rules of the Group
   Attendance
   Format
   Roles

5. Stating the Purpose of the Treatment and Group

6. Exploring Clients' Expectations and Concerns

7. Homework (Genogram/Family Tree)
   Describe the purpose of the Family Tree.
   Demonstrate using the example on the flipchart.
   Hand out folder packages.

8. Check-out

TIPS **FOR INDIVIDUAL COUPLE SESSION**

There is no group orientation. The assessment and introduction sessions are incorporated into one session. This session may be longer than other sessions.

Read and follow applicable directions from checklists for both the Assessment and Session 1. Cover the following information from Session 1 (Introduction):

- Give information about participating in the program, topics, format, rules, confidentiality, hopes and expectations.

- In preparation for Session 2, describe the Genogram/Family Tree and the concept of homework.

- Set the next appointment and hand out the Family Tree for completion prior to the next session.

DESCRIPTION OF TOPICS

H

The topics to be covered over the eight sessions of this group:

Session	Date	Time	Topic
I			Introduction — Family Tree
2			Thinking about What Change Would Look Like (Miracle Question)
3			Goal Setting
4			Steps towards Achieving Goals
5			Communication I
6			Communication 2
7			Trust and Intimacy
8			Relapse Prevention

H   **FAMILY TREE GUIDELINES**

SYMBOL	REPRESENTS
□	male
○	female
——————	marriage or partnership
│	child
——/∤—	divorce or separation
◎ or ▣	person with drug or alcohol problem
– – – – –	distant relationship
═══════	close relationship
/////////////	conflict
⊗ or ⊠	death

Put age, or year of death, of each person in box.
Beside each box, put relevant information concerning:

Occupation	Offender
Physical health	Number of marriages, including common-law
Mental health	Country of origin
Addiction	Migration story
Victim of abuse	

SAMPLE FAMILY TREE

H

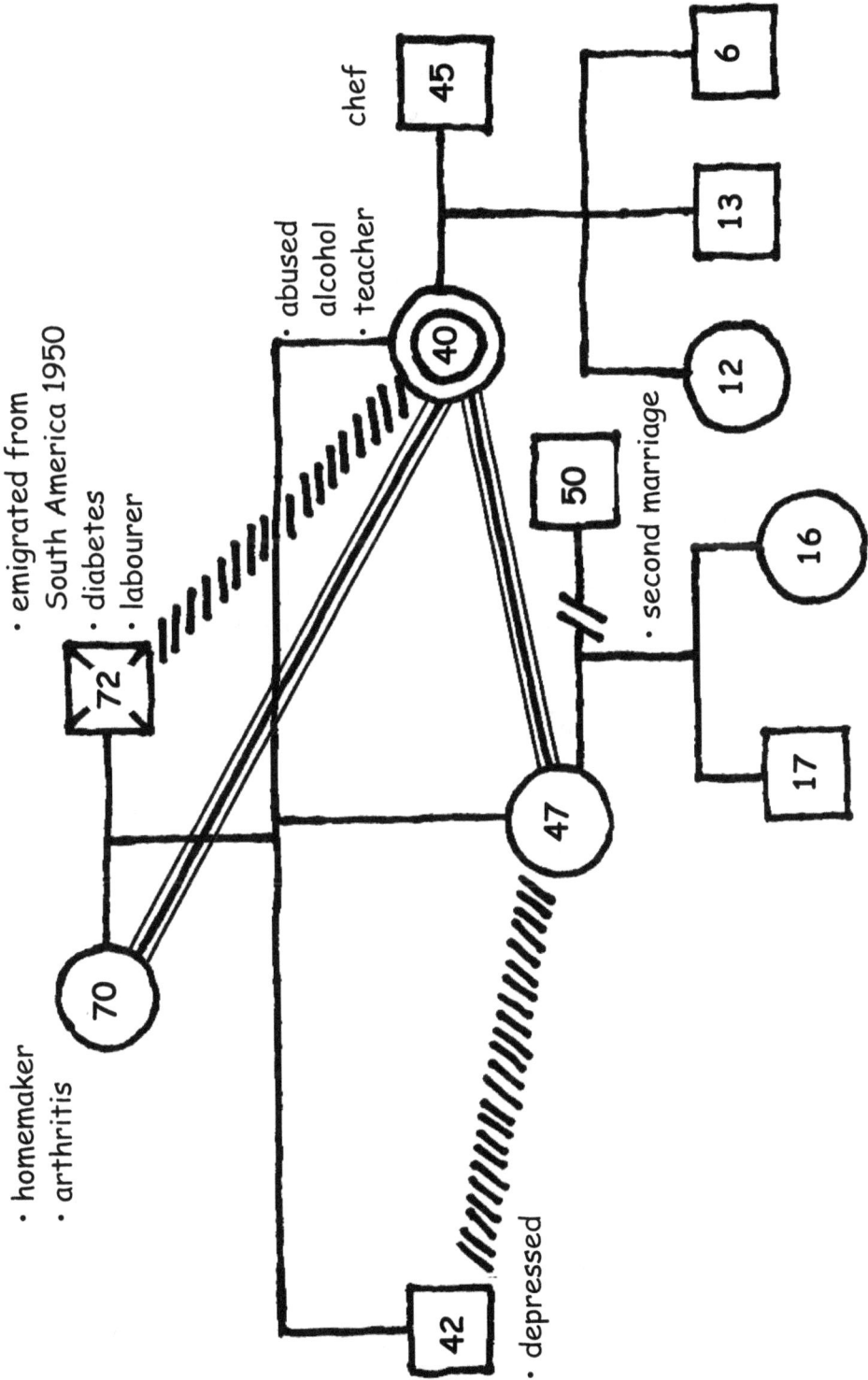

Put age or year of death of each person in box.

Progress Note: Introduction

Session date _____
DD/MM/YY

Patient/Client Name _____   Health Record # _____

☐ Patient/Client cancelled   Specify action plan _____
☐ No show   _____
☐ Therapist cancelled

☐ **Attended Session #1 of the BCT Program**

This session was conducted in the following format   ☐ Individual   ☐ Group

This session covered the following (check one box)

COVERED	NOT COVERED	
☐	☐	The program was introduced by the therapist(s)
☐	☐	Information about participating in the program and confidentiality was reviewed
☐	☐	Group topics, format and rules were reviewed
☐	☐	Introductions were made
☐	☐	Group members' hopes and expectations for the group were discussed
☐	☐	In preparation for session 2, genograms and concept of homework were introduced
☐	☐	Check-out completed

Drug Use Goal(s): ☐ Abstinent ☐ Reduction ☐ Undecided ☐ No change ☐ N/A
Substance Use Since Last Session: ☐ Abstinent ☐ Non-abstinent ☐ Don't know ☐ N/A

_____
_____

Therapists (print name & credentials):
(for group only)
1. _____
2. _____

Outcome of Session:
☐ Next Session Scheduled for: _____
☐ Treatment Terminated (patient/client initiated)
☐ Treatment Terminated (therapist initiated)

Additional Notes:
_____
_____
_____
_____

FORM COMPLETED BY

_____   _____   _____
NAME (PRINT)   SIGNATURE AND CREDENTIALS   DATE

GENOGRAM/FAMILY TREE

Session **2**

Session Guidelines

Session Resources

Client Handouts

GENOGRAM/FAMILY TREE

Session Guidelines

OBJECTIVES
Couples will:
- begin to understand the impact of substance use on their own relationship and their families of origin
- begin to identify patterns of use and related problems in their own relationship
- further identify and develop their treatment goals.

Group cohesion and commitment will continue to develop.

CHECKLIST

Guidelines for the Counsellor	Tips on What to Do with or Say to the Client
1. Check-in	Ask about questions or issues arising from the last session. "Name a thought, word or feeling that describes how you are right now."
2. Stating the Format and Purpose of This Session	"Through the presentation of the family trees to the group, you will begin to understand the impact of substance use in your own relationship and in your families of origin. This will help you to focus on areas for change and relationship goals. We will begin this process tonight with a review of your family trees, and we will continue to explore goals and areas for change in later sessions."
3. Reviewing Family Trees	Each couple will present their family tree, which will be taped to the wall. All of the family trees will be explored with the group in terms of patterns of family relationships, and positive and negative aspects of these relationships. Group leaders will record common themes and issues on a flipchart, keeping in mind potential areas for change and treatment goals. To the extent that it is comfortable for the client who is sharing, explore relationship patterns, substance use, and similarities and differences across generations that may be influencing the current couple relationship. Ask couples to "identify two things of interest that helped you to do this — one pleasant surprise and one not-so-pleasant surprise."

4. Homework (Miracle Question)

Couples are instructed to complete the Miracle Question handout for discussion in the next session. Note that the purpose of the Miracle Question is to instil a sense of hope and agency in each individual. It is not to encourage one partner to try to change the other partner.

"This exercise will help you to create a future vision of your relationship. Please read each question, think about an answer and then write down your response. Each partner can have a different miracle. You will share your miracle with the group in our next meeting."

5. Check-out

Ask each group member to state one positive word that he or she is thinking or a feeling that he or she is experiencing. The therapist can begin with an example such as "I'm feeling hopeful."

Session Resources

MATERIALS

- tape for taping family trees to the wall or a stand to put up family tree flipcharts
  (Note: two stands would make it possible to put up flipcharts for both partners, side by side, for
  further comparison of patterns and themes.)
- Miracle Question homework sheet
  (Note: if a client is unable to write, or if English is not his or her first language, the client may use
  other methods to answer the Miracle Question, such as drawing symbols, writing in his or her
  first language or making brief notes to jog memory.)

SUMMARY

1. Check-in
   Discuss comments or issues arising from the last session.

2. Stating the Format and Purpose of This Session

3. Reviewing Family Trees
   Focus on areas of change and treatment goals.
   Review family trees.
   Allot sufficient time — approximately 10 minutes per person.
   Group leader(s) record common themes and issues on a flipchart — note potential
       treatment topics and goals.
   Explore patterns and themes with couples.
   Identify one pleasant surprise and one not-so-pleasant surprise.

4. Homework (Miracle Question)
   Describe the purpose of the Miracle Question.
   Explain how to do it — give examples of concrete miracles.
   Remind couples they will be sharing their miracles with the group.
   Hand out packages.

5. Check-out

TIPS **FOR INDIVIDUAL COUPLE SESSION**

- Check-in: Ask the couple to talk about anything that came up for them as a result of the previous session and then ask them about their week.

- Family Trees: Discussion about the couple's family trees is briefer in the individual sessions. Extra time can be used to explore more fully and concretely the impact of past family patterns on the substance use and on the present couple relationship. As well, extra time can be used to begin to look at possible changes that the couple might want to make in their relationship.

- Use the extra time to explore what pieces of the family history were known to the couple.

- Ask them if they learned anything new or surprising about their own family or about their partners.

THE MIRACLE QUESTION

After thinking about your relationship, please take a few moments to answer the following questions:

Suppose one night, while you were asleep, there was a miracle and your relationship issues were resolved. When you woke up:

• how would you know a miracle had occurred?

• what sorts of things would be different?

• how would *you be thinking* differently?

• what would *you be doing* differently?

• how would your family/friends know that a miracle had occurred?

You can provide as much detail as you need to describe what your life would be like after this miracle. Try to think about your miracle in concrete terms (e.g., "we will go for long walks together" or "after we put the children to bed, we will spend time cuddling on the couch and talking") as opposed to abstract wishes (e.g., "we will be happy").

Also, be sure to focus on **changes in your own behaviour** when you are describing changes in the relationship.

_____

_____

_____

_____

_____

_____

_____

_____

_____

Progress Note: Genogram/Family Tree

Session date _____
DD/MM/YY

Patient/Client Name _____   Health Record # _____

□ Patient/Client cancelled   Specify action plan _____
□ No show   _____
□ Therapist cancelled

□ **Attended Session #2 of the BCT Program**

This session was conducted in the following format   □ Individual   □ Group

This session covered the following (check one box)

COVERED	NOT COVERED	
□	□	Patient/Client homework of genograms was reviewed
□	□	Patient/Client discussed preliminary short- and long-term treatment goals
□	□	Homework assigned: _____
□	□	Check-out completed

Drug Use Goal(s):   □ Abstinent   □ Reduction   □ Undecided   □ No change   □ N/A
Substance Use Since Last Session: □ Abstinent   □ Non-abstinent   □ Don't know   □ N/A

_____
_____

Therapists (print name & credentials):
(for group only)
1. _____
2. _____

Outcome of Session:
□ Next Session Scheduled for: _____
□ Treatment Terminated (patient/client initiated)
□ Treatment Terminated (therapist initiated)

Additional Notes:
_____
_____
_____
_____

FORM COMPLETED BY

_____   _____   _____
NAME (PRINT)   SIGNATURE AND CREDENTIALS   DATE

MIRACLE QUESTION

Session 3

MIRACLE QUESTION

Session Guidelines

OBJECTIVES
Couples will begin to:
- identify any positive small changes within their relationship
- focus on the future and form a vision of how they would like the relationship to be
- focus on reasonable and achievable goals that will bring them closer to their vision.

CHECKLIST

Guidelines for the Counsellor	Tips on What to Do with or Say to the Client
1. Check-in	Ask about issues arising from the last session. "Name a thought, word or feeling that describes how you are right now."
2. Stating the Format and Purpose of This Session	"By reviewing the miracles that you've written down, we hope to help you formulate a vision of how you would like your relationship to be, and communicate this to your partner and the group."
3. Reviewing Miracle Question Homework	Ask couples to discuss their miracles. They may need help keeping the focus of the discussion on themselves, rather than their partners, and on concrete changes. Encourage concrete, specific and behavioural answers; specifically, ask them what would they be doing differently and not how they would be feeling different. Therapists should listen for small, concrete expressions (e.g., we would kiss each other goodbye when we leave for work). Ask people if any part of their miracle is already happening, and if so, what is that like?
4. Homework (Goal Assignment 1)	Couples are instructed to complete the Goal Assignment 1 sheet for discussion in the next session. Couples will individually select a personal goal and a couple goal from their miracle, and write down the steps needed to achieve that goal. Therapists should encourage positive, action-oriented goals (e.g., "talk twice a week" versus "argue less") and give clients examples of individual goals (e.g., "I want

to handle problems more calmly") and couple goals (e.g., "we will go for a walk together once a week"). Instruct them to be specific in identifying steps that will help them move towards their goal.

5. Check-out

Ask each group member to offer one positive word, thought or message that he or she got out of the session.

Session Resources

MATERIALS
- pens and copies of Miracle Question exercise
- homework sheets: Goal Assignment 1

SUMMARY

1. Check-in
   Ask about comments or issues arising from the last session.
   Ask participants to express a thought, word or feeling.

2. Stating the Format and Purpose of This Session
   Miracle Question

3. Reviewing Miracle Question Homework
   Ask couples to discuss their miracles.
   Encourage clients to focus on themselves and to be concrete and specific.
   There are no right or wrong answers — couples may interpret the "miracle" differently.

4. Homework (Goal Assignment 1)
   Describe the purpose of Goal Assignment 1.
   Explain how. Give examples. Remind clients to think of steps towards goals.
   Hand out packages.

5. Check-out

TIPS FOR INDIVIDUAL COUPLE SESSION 3

- During the session, it is important to stress to clients that their miracle should be specific, concrete, behavioural and about themselves, not their partner. Redirect clients to focus on the concrete, behavioural elements of the miracle if they get sidetracked.

- Because there is more time than in the group format, therapists should ensure that partners have heard and understood each other's miracle. Use this time also to clarify and explore what each would be doing differently.

H   GOAL ASSIGNMENT 1

Based on today's discussion, we would like you to think about what you want to be different, both for yourself and in your relationship.

Please select a personal goal for yourself and a goal as a couple, and also note some of the steps that would help you to achieve the miracle:

(Try to choose small, concrete and specific goals. The couple goal should not involve changing the other partner.)

Personal Goal for Yourself	Goal as a Couple

Steps to Achieve Goal	Steps to Achieve Goal

Progress Note: Miracle Question

Session date _____
DD/MM/YY

Patient/Client Name _____ Health Record # _____

☐ Patient/Client cancelled   Specify action plan _____
☐ No show   _____
☐ Therapist cancelled

☐ **Attended Session #3 of the BCT Program**
This session was conducted in the following format   ☐ Individual   ☐ Group
This session covered the following (check one box)

	NOT	
COVERED	COVERED	
☐	☐	Homework reviewed
☐	☐	Miracle question exercise completed and discussed
☐	☐	Homework assigned: _____
☐	☐	Check-out completed

Drug Use Goal(s):   ☐ Abstinent   ☐ Reduction   ☐ Undecided   ☐ No change   ☐ N/A
Substance Use Since Last Session: ☐ Abstinent   ☐ Non-abstinent   ☐ Don't know   ☐ N/A

_____
_____

Therapists (print name & credentials):
(for group only)
1. _____
2. _____

Outcome of Session:
☐ Next Session Scheduled for: _____
☐ Treatment Terminated (patient/client initiated)
☐ Treatment Terminated (therapist initiated)

Additional Notes:
_____
_____
_____
_____

FORM COMPLETED BY

_____ _____ _____
NAME (PRINT)   SIGNATURE AND CREDENTIALS   DATE

GOAL SETTING

Session Guidelines

Session Resources

Client Handouts

GOAL SETTING

Session Guidelines

OBJECTIVES
Each partner will:
- select one personal goal and one couple goal
- identify the steps needed to achieve his or her goals

Couples will have begun the process of engaging in the negotiation of their goals with each other.

Group cohesion and commitment will continue to develop.

CHECKLIST

Guidelines for the Counsellor	Tips on What to Do with or Say to the Client
1. Check-in	Ask about issues arising from the last session.
	"Name a thought, word or feeling that describes how you are right now."
2. Stating the Format and Purpose of This Session	"In today's session, we are going to be working on personal and couple goals. As facilitators, we will give you some feedback as you discuss your goals, and it may also be helpful for group members to give each other feedback on goals and on goal setting as we go along."
3. Reviewing Goal Assignment 1 Homework	Ask each member to share his or her goals with the group. Have him or her scale the goals (1-10) in terms of how close each goal is to being achieved. Also, note where there are common goals among group members. Some time for discussion and group feedback may be required when a couple's goals conflict.
	Ask couples to choose a goal to work on together.
	Encourage them to choose a goal that is clear, concrete and attainable, and point out that goal achievement is a step-by-step process. Ask couples to identify some of the steps that will be required to achieve their goals. Feedback from other group members may help couples establish these steps.

4. Homework (Goal Assignment 2)

Couples are instructed to complete the Goal Assignment 2 sheet for discussion in the next session. "Next week, we will review your progress and we will do an exercise designed to help you work on your goals with your partner."

(Therapists keep notes of each client's goals to be reviewed in Session 7.)

5. Check-out

Ask each group member to state one positive word that he or she is thinking or a feeling that he or she is experiencing.

Session Resources

MATERIALS
- pens
- homework sheets: Goal Assignment 2

SUMMARY

1. Check-in
   Name a thought/word/feeling and/or discuss issues arising from the last session.

2. Stating the Format and Purpose of This Session

3. Reviewing Goal Assignment 1 Homework
   Each group member shares personal goals and couple goals.
   Have each client prioritize goals and choose one attainable goal.
   Help couples work out the steps needed to attain goals.

4. Homework (Goal Assignment 2)
   Hand out Goal Assignment 2 sheet. Instruct couples to complete it for next session.

5. Check-out

TIPS FOR INDIVIDUAL COUPLE SESSION 4

- Use extra time to clarify goals, both personal and couple, that are small, concrete, attainable and specific.

- Stress that goals should be about themselves and should not involve changing the other partner.

- Encourage clients to frame their goals in a positive, action-oriented way (i.e., "our goal is to talk twice a week" versus "our goal is to argue less").

H   **GOAL ASSIGNMENT 2**

1. Select a goal that you have identified through today's discussion and that you will work on **during the coming week**.

    _____

    _____

    _____

2. On a scale of 1 to 10, circle how close you are to achieving this goal **now**.

    NOT
    ACHIEVED
    AT ALL   FULLY
                                                             ACHIEVED

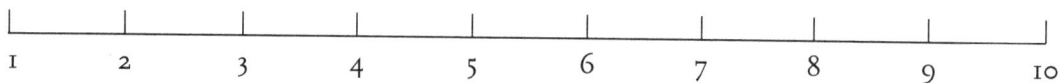

    | | | | | | | | | | |
    1   2   3   4   5   6   7   8   9   10

3. List specific steps you plan to take towards this goal.

    _____

    _____

    _____

4. List progress/steps that you have taken over the course of the week.

    _____

    _____

    _____

5. On a scale of 1 to 10, circle how close you are to achieving this goal **at the end of the week**.

    NOT
    ACHIEVED
    AT ALL   FULLY
                                                             ACHIEVED

    | | | | | | | | | | |
    1   2   3   4   5   6   7   8   9   10

Progress Note: Goal Setting

Session date _____
DD/MM/YY

Patient/Client Name _____   Health Record # _____

☐ Patient/Client cancelled   Specify action plan _____
☐ No show   _____
☐ Therapist cancelled

☐ **Attended Session #4 of the BCT Program**
This session was conducted in the following format   ☐ Individual   ☐ Group
This session covered the following (check one box)

NOT		
COVERED	COVERED	
☐	☐	Goals based on homework discussed
☐	☐	Individual goal(s) identified
☐	☐	Couple goal(s) identified
☐	☐	Homework assigned: _____
☐	☐	Check-out completed

Drug Use Goal(s):   ☐ Abstinent   ☐ Reduction   ☐ Undecided   ☐ No change   ☐ N/A
Substance Use Since Last Session: ☐ Abstinent   ☐ Non-abstinent   ☐ Don't know   ☐ N/A

_____
_____

Therapists (print name & credentials):
(for group only)
1. _____
2. _____

Outcome of Session:
☐ Next Session Scheduled for: _____
☐ Treatment Terminated (patient/client initiated)
☐ Treatment Terminated (therapist initiated)

Additional Notes:
_____
_____
_____
_____

FORM COMPLETED BY

_____   _____   _____
NAME (PRINT)   SIGNATURE AND CREDENTIALS   DATE

COMMUNICATION

Session 5

Session Guidelines

Session Resources

Client Handouts

Progress Note

COMMUNICATION

Session **5**

Session Guidelines

OBJECTIVES
Couples will:
- start the process of working towards improving their communication within their relationship
- start to work on improving their listening and speaking skills
- identify the areas of deficiency that they would like to improve.

Individuals will practise listening and speaking skills and get feedback regarding what they did well and what to improve from their partners and from the group.

CHECKLIST

Guidelines for the Counsellor	Tips on What to Do with or Say to the Client
1. Check-in	Ask about issues arising from the last session. "Name a thought, word or feeling that describes how you are right now."
2. Stating the Format and Purpose of This Session	"The purpose of the session is for couples to learn or improve communication skills. In order to do this, look at the steps (listed in the Listening and Speaking Skills handout) that we would like you to use in order to express yourself."
3. Reviewing Session Homework	Discuss progress over the last week. Discuss the steps and progress that each person has made towards working on his or her goals. Therapists keep track of client goals and progress for later sessions.
4. Role Plays	Give out the Listening and Speaking Skills exercise. Based on issues or goals that couples defined in previous sessions, have them practise role plays using the Listening and Speaking Skills exercise to help improve their communicating within the relationship. **OPTIONS** a) If time does not permit each couple to practise role plays, and if couples have varying skill levels, choose one couple to practise in front of the group.

	b) Therapists choose a topic and role-play effective communication on that topic for the group. c) Do one role-play exercise with speaking skills only, followed by a role play with listening skills only, followed by both.
5. Homework (Listening and Speaking Skills)	Couples are asked to continue working on Listening and Speaking Skills before the next session.
6. Check-out	Ask each group member to state one positive word that he or she is thinking or a feeling that he or she is experiencing.

Session Resources

MATERIALS
• pens and copies of Listening and Speaking Skills exercise

SUMMARY

---

1. Check-in
   Name a thought/word/feeling and/or discuss issues arising from the last session.

2. Stating the Format and Purpose of This Session

3. Reviewing Homework
   Keep track of client goals for later sessions.

4. Role Play and Practising Communication Skills
   Hand out Listening and Speaking Skills exercise.

5. Homework (Listening and Speaking Skills)

6. Check-out

TIPS FOR INDIVIDUAL COUPLE SESSION 5

Use extra time to prioritize both personal and couple goals and to discuss specific steps in planning to achieve these goals.

Have couples begin to practise listening and speaking skills in role-play discussions.

H   LISTENING AND SPEAKING SKILLS

Use this handout to help you practise listening and speaking skills. These skills are important parts of communication in any relationship. They are particularly helpful when speaking with your partner. The use of active listening skills may help you better understand what your partner is trying to tell you about his or her own feelings and thoughts. Using "I" language lets your partner know how you feel about something, when you feel that way, why you feel that way and how you would like things to be.

Active Listening:

1. Look at the other person. Make eye contact.
2. Show the person you understand by nodding your head and looking interested.
3. Ask questions when you want more information or when you don't understand.
4. Repeat, in your own words, what the other person has said. Then she or he will be able to let you know if you understood what was said.
5. Show that you want to hear what the other person has to say.
6. Don't give advice unless you are asked for advice.
7. Although you may not agree with the other person, respect his or her point of view.

"I" Statements:

1. Use "I" statements to talk about your feelings.
2. Say one thing at a time.
3. When describing your reaction to something another person has said or done, focus on the behaviour of the other person, not the whole person.
4. Try not to use general statements like "you never" or "you always." Be very specific.
5. Be positive.

EXAMPLE

"**I feel** frustrated **when you** drop your laundry on the floor. **I would prefer** that you put it in the hamper."

A. Practise using "I" statements in the following format:

I feel _____ (emotion)

When you _____ (behaviour)

I would prefer _____ (specify need)

B. Practise using "I" statements in different ways, making sure to identify your own emotions and/or your needs. When talking about your partner, be sure to specify your partner's behaviour(s).

LISTENING AND SPEAKING SKILLS PRACTICE DIARY*

H

Name	Date	Time	Listening Skills	Speaking Skills	Outcome
			☐	☐	
			☐	☐	
			☐	☐	
			☐	☐	
			☐	☐	
			☐	☐	
			☐	☐	
			☐	☐	
			☐	☐	
			☐	☐	
			☐	☐	
			☐	☐	

*Each time you practise using listening and speaking skills this week, complete this Practice Diary, filling out the date and time, which skill(s) you practised, and any comments about how it turned out. Bring it with you for discussion next week.

Progress Note: Communication

Session date   _____
             DD/MM/YY

Patient/Client Name   _____   Health Record #   _____

☐ Patient/Client cancelled   Specify action plan   _____
☐ No show
☐ Therapist cancelled   _____

☐ **Attended Session #5 of the BCT Program**

This session was conducted in the following format   ☐ Individual   ☐ Group

This session covered the following (check one box)

COVERED	NOT COVERED	
☐	☐	Patient/Client completed "check-in" and reviewed homework
☐	☐	Therapist(s) introduced Listening and Speaking Skills exercise
☐	☐	Listening and Speaking Skills exercise completed and discussed
☐	☐	Homework assigned: _____
☐	☐	Check-out completed

Drug Use Goal(s):   ☐ Abstinent   ☐ Reduction   ☐ Undecided   ☐ No change   ☐ N/A

Substance Use Since Last Session: ☐ Abstinent   ☐ Non-abstinent   ☐ Don't know   ☐ N/A

_____

_____

Therapists (print name & credentials):
(for group only)

1. _____

2. _____

Outcome of Session:

☐ Next Session Scheduled for: _____

☐ Treatment Terminated (patient/client initiated)

☐ Treatment Terminated (therapist initiated)

Additional Notes:

_____

_____

_____

_____

FORM COMPLETED BY

_____   _____   _____
NAME (PRINT)   SIGNATURE AND CREDENTIALS   DATE

TRUST/INTIMACY

Session Guidelines

Session Resources

Client Handouts

Progress Note

Session Guidelines

OBJECTIVES

Couples will:

- continue to work towards improving their communication within their relationship
- continue to work on expressing their thoughts and feelings to their partners
- practise expressing their thoughts and feelings to their partners and get feedback from the group.
- begin to work on building trust and intimacy.

CHECKLIST

Guidelines for the Counsellor	Tips on What to Do with or Say to the Client
1. Check-in	Ask about issues arising from the last session. "Name a thought, word or feeling that describes how you are right now."
2. Stating the Format and Purpose of This Session	"The purpose of the session is to review your homework and continue to work on improving your communication skills. We will also discuss the concepts of trust and intimacy."
3. Reviewing Session Homework	Discuss progress on listening and speaking skills development over the last week. Hand out Tips for Effective Communication to facilitate further practice.
4. Practising Role Plays	Participants are asked to continue to practise role plays. These can be based on participants' homework. Encourage the use of "I" language and feedback from other members as each couple takes a turn practising role-play discussions.
5. Homework (Trust/Intimacy)	Discuss the meaning of trust and intimacy before handing out the exercise: "Trust is important in a relationship. There may be areas where there is no trust. There are probably also areas where there is more or a lot of trust." "We express intimacy in various ways (e.g., interacting physically; sharing thoughts/feelings; taking care of each other; spending time together...). Trust and

intimacy are often connected and people need to have trust in order to express intimacy."

Therapist may have couples brainstorm a list about what trust and intimacy mean to them. Put this list on the board.

Hand out the Trust/Intimacy assignment for couples to work on before the next session.

---

6. Check-out

Ask each group member to state one positive word that he or she is thinking or a feeling that he or she is experiencing.

Session Resources

MATERIALS
- pens and copies of Trust/Intimacy exercise
- copies of Tips for Effective Communication

SUMMARY

1. Check-in
   Discuss thought/word/feeling and/or issues arising from the last session.

2. Stating the Format and Purpose of This Session
   Continue to improve communication skills.

3. Reviewing Session Homework and Practising Communication Skills
   Discuss progress on listening and speaking skills.
   Hand out Tips for Effective Communication.

4. Practising Role Plays
   Encourage the use of "I" language.
   Each couple takes a turn practising role play.

5. Handing Out Homework (Trust/Intimacy)
   Discuss meaning of trust and intimacy before handing out exercise.

6. Check-out

TIPS FOR INDIVIDUAL COUPLE SESSION 6

- Ask the couple for a specific situation that they could role-play using listening and speaking skills.

- Encourage the use of "I" language.

H TIPS FOR EFFECTIVE COMMUNICATION

Three basic skills of good communication are:

- looking

- listening and

- speaking.

Looking

Look at the other person. Make eye contact.

Pay attention to body language, such as facial expression and gestures. These things help you to understand what the other person is expressing.

Show that you are listening by leaning forward, nodding your head, looking interested and using encouraging phrases, such as "uh-huh," "go on" or "I see what you mean."

Listening

Pay attention.

Ask questions when you want more information or don't understand.

Repeat, in your own words, what the other person has said. Then she or he will be able to let you know if you understood what was said.

Don't think ahead to what you are going to say. Don't rehearse what you want to say while the other is speaking.

Don't interrupt. Remain silent when the other person speaks.

Show that you want to hear what the other person has to say.

Speaking

Use "I" statements.

FOR EXAMPLE:
"I feel _____, when you _____, I would prefer _____."

Be very specific. Steer clear of general statements, like "you never..." or "you always...."

Be honest about what you are thinking and feeling.

Avoid blaming, name-calling or advice-giving (unless the other person asks for your advice).

Focus on the issue at hand — don't bring past arguments and issues into the current discussion.

H

Be positive and solution-focused.

Although you may not agree with the other person, respect his or her point of view.

Other Hints

If the discussion escalates into an argument, take a break.

Make sure you agree on a time when you will come back to the discussion when you are both feeling calmer.

Sometimes, it is easier to have a difficult conversation in a new or different location (e.g., outside the home, in a coffee shop, etc.).

Practise talking about less difficult (or less "loaded") issues first.

Be sure to spend time talking about positive things each day.

H   **TRUST/INTIMACY EXERCISE**

In your relationship, list three areas where trust is important to you:

A. _____

B. _____

C. _____

On a scale from 1 to 10, please rate how much trust there is in each of these areas:

A.   NOT   A GREAT
     A LOT OF   DEAL OF
     TRUST   TRUST

     1   2   3   4   5   6   7   8   9   10

B.   NOT   A GREAT
     A LOT OF   DEAL OF
     TRUST   TRUST

     1   2   3   4   5   6   7   8   9   10

C.   NOT   A GREAT
     A LOT OF   DEAL OF
     TRUST   TRUST

     1   2   3   4   5   6   7   8   9   10

What are some specific ways that you express intimacy and caring in your relationship?

_____

_____

_____

What are some steps to building trust and intimacy in your relationship?

_____

_____

_____

Progress Note: Trust/Intimacy

Session date _____
DD/MM/YY

Patient/Client Name _____   Health Record # _____

☐ Patient/Client cancelled   Specify action plan _____
☐ No show   _____
☐ Therapist cancelled

☐ **Attended Session #6 of the BCT Program**
This session was conducted in the following format   ☐ Individual   ☐ Group
This session covered the following (check one box)

COVERED	NOT COVERED	
☐	☐	Patient/Client completed "check-in" and reviewed homework
☐	☐	Therapist(s) introduced trust/intimacy exercise
☐	☐	Trust/intimacy exercise completed and discussed
☐	☐	Explored the issue of trust in the couple's relationship and the way that it can be addressed
☐	☐	Discussed ways to build trust and express caring in relationship
☐	☐	Homework assigned: _____
☐	☐	Check-out completed

Drug Use Goal(s):   ☐ Abstinent   ☐ Reduction   ☐ Undecided   ☐ No change   ☐ N/A
Substance Use Since Last Session: ☐ Abstinent   ☐ Non-abstinent   ☐ Don't know   ☐ N/A

_____
_____

Therapists (print name & credentials):
(for group only)
1. _____
2. _____

Outcome of Session:
☐ Next Session Scheduled for: _____
☐ Treatment Terminated (patient/client initiated)
☐ Treatment Terminated (therapist initiated)

Additional Notes:
_____
_____
_____

FORM COMPLETED BY

_____   _____   _____
NAME (PRINT)   SIGNATURE AND CREDENTIALS   DATE

RELAPSE PREVENTION

Session 7

Session Guidelines

OBJECTIVES

Couples will:
- continue to work towards improving their communication within their relationship
- continue building trust and intimacy
- begin to think about and define areas of relapse and relapse prevention.

CHECKLIST

Guidelines for the Counsellor	Tips on What to Do with or Say to the Client
1. Check-in	Ask about issues arising from the last session. "Name a thought, word or feeling that describes how you are right now."
2. Stating the Format and Purpose of This Session	"The purpose of the session is for members to discuss trust and intimacy. The homework will focus on relapse prevention."
3. Reviewing Session Homework	Discuss progress on issues related to trust and intimacy. Ask couples to talk about areas of trust and the degree of trust in their relationships. Put the emphasis on breaking issues into small, concrete steps, focusing on how couples can move forward in an active way.
4. Homework (Relapse Prevention/ Maintenance)	The focus of relapse prevention will be defined by couples' issues discussed over the course of the therapy, such as the return to former patterns of behaviour, including substance use and its potential impact on the relationship. Hand out sheets with the following questions: • What is a relapse for you as a couple (e.g., communication breakdown; loss of trust; loss of intimacy, etc.)? • What would be the clues that a relapse has happened? • Describe a plan for preventing relapse. Be specific. Discuss the questions with the group members.
5. Check-out	Ask each group member to state one positive word that he or she is thinking or a feeling that he or she is experiencing.

Session Resources

MATERIALS

• pens and copies of Relapse Prevention exercise.

SUMMARY

1. Check-in
   Name a thought/word/feeling and/or discuss issues arising from the last session.

2. Stating the Format and Purpose of This Session
   Discuss trust and intimacy.
   Begin to think about possible plans for relapse prevention.

3. Reviewing Session Homework
   Discuss issues related to trust and intimacy.

4. Introducing, Describing and Handing Out Relapse Prevention Exercise

5. Check-out

TIPS FOR INDIVIDUAL COUPLE SESSION 7

• Use the time to explore and discuss issues relating to trust and intimacy.

RELAPSE PREVENTIONMAINTENANCE

What is a relapse for you as a couple (e.g., communication breakdown, loss of trust, loss of intimacy, etc.)?

_____

_____

_____

_____

_____

What would be the clues that a relapse might happen?

_____

_____

_____

_____

_____

Outline a plan for preventing relapse — be specific!

_____

_____

_____

_____

_____

Progress Note: Relapse Prevention

Session date _____
DD/MM/YY

Patient/Client Name _____   Health Record # _____

☐ Patient/Client cancelled
☐ No show
☐ Therapist cancelled

Specify action plan _____
_____

☐ **Attended Session #7 of the BCT Program**

This session was conducted in the following format   ☐ Individual   ☐ Group

This session covered the following (check one box)

COVERED	NOT COVERED	
☐	☐	Patient/Client completed "check-in" and reviewed homework
☐	☐	Therapist(s) introduced relapse prevention plan
☐	☐	Relapse prevention plan exercise completed
☐	☐	Discussed ways to cope with relapse and reviewed action plans
☐	☐	Homework assigned: _____
☐	☐	Check-out completed

Drug Use Goal(s):   ☐ Abstinent   ☐ Reduction   ☐ Undecided   ☐ No change   ☐ N/A

Substance Use Since Last Session: ☐ Abstinent   ☐ Non-abstinent   ☐ Don't know   ☐ N/A

_____
_____

Therapists (print name & credentials):
(for group only)

1. _____
2. _____

Outcome of Session:

☐ Next Session Scheduled for: _____
☐ Treatment Terminated (patient/client initiated)
☐ Treatment Terminated (therapist initiated)

Additional Notes:

_____
_____
_____

FORM COMPLETED BY

_____   _____   _____
NAME (PRINT)   SIGNATURE AND CREDENTIALS   DATE

CONCLUSION

Session **8**

Session Guidelines

Session Resources

Session Guidelines

OBJECTIVES
- Summary session of issues and work done — couples will review major issues and goals.
- Couples will work on future goals and plans to prevent lapsing into problem patterns.

CHECKLIST

Guidelines for the Counsellor	Tips on What to Do with or Say to the Client
1. Check-in	Ask about issues arising from the last session. "Name a thought, word or feeling that describes how you are right now."
2. Stating the Format and Purpose of This Session	"The purpose of this group is 1) to review the major issues and goals; 2) to normalize/formalize the ending process; 3) to plan future goals and how you can avoid returning to old patterns that are unhelpful or problematic." Some of the issues discussed over the past eight weeks include goal identification, drug use patterns and impact, building trust/intimacy, coping with differences/conflicts and relapse planning. It is important to keep in mind that the end of any program may bring out a range of feelings (e.g., sadness, joy, anxiety and relief) both in the participant and in the therapist. The ending of this group can be viewed as a transition or a new beginning for the couples and their relationship; it is a chance to follow through on the change process that they have started by attending the Brief Couples Therapy (BCT) program.
3. Reviewing Homework	Discuss relapse prevention plans. Raise issues about how a relapse could be handled and its impact on the relationship.
4. Homework (Imagining Changes Six Months from Now)	Ask the participants the following question: "Let's pretend it is six months later. What would you like to be able to report about changes in your relationship?" Based on what the participants talk about, point out that this is what they can then work on for the next

	six months. What they have selected can be their vision or miracle, and they can then continue to work on it as if they were returning. The therapist may summarize and underscore progress made over the course of therapy.
5. Obtaining Feedback on Treatment	"What was most helpful about the treatment?" "Do you have any suggestions on how to improve these sessions?" Therapists take notes on clients' feedback.
6. Check-out	Give a Gift: imagine that there is a box of all sorts of gifts on the table before you. I'd like you to take a minute and think of one tangible and one intangible gift that you would like to take and give to the person on your right.

Session Resources

MATERIALS
• pens and copies of exercises or notes from previous sessions

SUMMARY

1. Check-in
   Name a thought/word/feeling and/or discuss issues arising from the last session.

2. Stating the Format and Purpose of This Session
   Review goals and issues.
   Plan to avoid negative patterns and habits.
   Plan for the future.

3. Reviewing Relapse Prevention/Maintenance homework

4. Homework (Imagine Changes Six Months from Now)

5. Obtaining Feedback on Treatment

6. Check-out
   Give a Gift exercise

TIPS FOR INDIVIDUAL COUPLE SESSION 8

• Use the time for summarizing and highlighting progress achieved during the sessions.

• Discuss how the couple can avoid relapsing into negative patterns and habits.

• Checkout: ask the couple to identify one "hope" they have for themselves as a couple.

Progress Note: Conclusion

Session date _____
DD/MM/YY

Patient/Client Name _____ Health Record # _____

☐ Patient/Client cancelled   Specify action plan _____
☐ No show   _____
☐ Therapist cancelled

☐ **Attended Session #8 of the BCT Program**
This session was conducted in the following format   ☐ Individual   ☐ Group
This session covered the following (check one box)

COVERED	NOT COVERED	
☐	☐	Patient/Client completed "check-in" and reviewed homework
☐	☐	Therapist(s) initiated review of group's progress from previous sessions
☐	☐	Discussed and celebrated work accomplished by participants
☐	☐	Future focus exercise completed and discussed
☐	☐	Group members were congratulated and thanked for their participation in the group
☐	☐	Check-out completed

Drug Use Goal(s):   ☐ Abstinent   ☐ Reduction   ☐ Undecided   ☐ No change   ☐ N/A
Substance Use Since Last Session: ☐ Abstinent   ☐ Non-abstinent   ☐ Don't know   ☐ N/A

_____
_____

Therapists (print name & credentials):
(for group only)
1. _____
2. _____

Outcome of Session:
☐ Next Session Scheduled for: _____
☐ Treatment Terminated (patient/client initiated)
☐ Treatment Terminated (therapist initiated)

Additional Notes:
_____
_____
_____

FORM COMPLETED BY

_____   _____   _____
NAME (PRINT)   SIGNATURE AND CREDENTIALS   DATE

REERENCES

Antony, M.M. & Swinson, R.P. (1996). *The Anxiety Disorders and Their Treatment: A Critical Analysis of the Literature on Effective Treatments.* Ottawa: Health Canada.

Bandura, A. & Walters, R.H. (1963). *Social Learning and Personality Development.* New York: Holt, Rinehart & Winston.

Baucom, D.H., Shoham, V., Mueser, K.T., Daiuto, A.D. & Stickle, T.R. (1998). Empirically supported couple and family interventions for marital distress and adult mental health problems. *Journal of Consulting and Clinical Psychology, 66(1),* 53-88.

Beck, A. (1976). *Cognitive Therapy and the Emotional Disorders.* New York: International Universities Press.

Berg, I.K. & Miller, S.D. (1992). *Working with the Problem Drinker: A Solution-Focused Approach.* New York: W.W. Norton.

Bowen, M. (1978). *Family Therapy in Clinical Practice.* New York: Jason Aronson.

Bowers, T.G. & Al-Redha, M.R. (1990). A comparison of outcome with group/marital and standard/individual therapies with alcoholics. *Journal of Studies on Alcohol, 51,* 301-309.

Cadogan, D.A. (1973). Marital group therapy in the treatment of alcoholism. *Quarterly Journal of Studies on Alcohol, 34,* 1187-1194.

Coché, J. (1995). Group therapy with couples. In N.S. Jacobson & A.S. Gurman (Eds.), *Clinical Handbook of Couple Therapy.* New York: Guilford.

Corder, B.F., Corder, R.F. & Laidlaw, N.D. (1972). An intensive treatment program for alcoholics and their wives. *Quarterly Journal of Studies on Alcohol, 33,* 1144-1146.

Daley, D.C. & Moss, H.B. (2002). *Dual Disorders: Counseling Clients with Chemical Dependency and Mental Illness.* Center City, Minn.: Hazelden.

Dobson, K.S. (1989). A meta-analysis of the efficacy of cognitive therapy for depression. *Journal of Consulting and Clinical Psychology, 57,* 414-419.

Edwards, M.E. & Steinglass, P. (1995). Family therapy treatment outcomes for alcoholism. *Journal of Marital and Family Therapy, 21(4),* 475-509.

Epstein, E.E. & McCrady, B.S. (1998). Behavioral couples treatment of alcohol and drug use disorders: Current status and innovations. *Clinical Psychology Review, 18(6),* 689-711.

Fals-Stewart, W., Birchler, G.R. & O'Farrell, T.J. (1996). Behavioral couples therapy for male substance-abusing patients: Effects on relationship adjustment and drug-using behavior. *Journal of Consulting and Clinical Psychology, 64(5),* 959-972.

Feld, B.G. (1997). An object relations perspective on couples group therapy. *International Journal of Group Psychotherapy, 47,* 315-332.

Feld, B.G. (1998). Initiating a couples group. *Group, 22,* 245-259.

Hahlweg, K., Revenstorf, D. & Schindler, L. (1982). Treatment of marital distress: Comparing formats and modalities. *Advances in Behaviour Research and Therapy, 4,* 57-74.

Haley, J. (1976). *Problem-Solving Therapy: New Strategies for Effective Family Therapy.* San Francisco: Jossey-Bass.

Kaufman, E. (1985). Family systems and family therapy of substance abuse: An overview of two decades of research and clinical experience. *The International Journal of the Addictions, 20(6&7)*, 897-916.

Lakoff, R.S. & Baggaley, A. (1994). Working with couples in a group: Theoretical and practical issues. *Group Analysis, 27*, 183-196.

Laszloffy, T.A. (2000). The implications of client satisfaction feedback for beginning family therapists: Back to the basics. *Journal of Marital and Family Therapy, 26(3)*, 391-397.

McCollum, E.E. & Trepper, T.S. (2001). *Family Solutions for Substance Abuse*. New York: Haworth Press.

McCrady, B.S., Paolino Jr., T.J., Longabough, R. & Rossi, J. (1979). Effects of joint hospital admission and couples treatment for hospitalized alcoholics: A pilot study. *Addictive Behaviours, 4*, 155-165.

Miller, W.R. & Rollnick, S. (1991). *Motivational Interviewing: Preparing People to Change Addictive Behavior*. New York: Guilford.

Minuchin, S. (1974). *Families and Family Therapy*. Cambridge, Mass.: Harvard University Press.

Montag, K.R. & Wilson, G.L. (1992). An empirical evaluation of behavioral and cognitive-behavioral group marital treatments with discordant couples. *Journal of Sex and Marital Therapy, 18(4)*, 255-272.

Nichols, M. & Schwartz, R.C. (1998). *Family Therapy: Concepts & Methods* (4th ed.). Needham Heights: Allyn & Bacon.

O'Farrell, T.J. (1993). A behavioral marital therapy couples group program for alcoholics and their spouses. In T.J. O'Farrell & W.R. Miller (Eds.), *Treating Alcohol Problems: Marital and Family Interventions* (pp. 170-209). New York: Guilford.

O'Farrell, T.J. (1995). Marital and family therapy. In R. Hester & W.R. Miller (Eds.), *Handbook of Alcoholism Treatment Approaches* (2nd ed., pp. 195-220). Boston: Allyn & Bacon.

O'Farrell, T.J., Choquette, K.A. & Cutter, H.S.G. (1998). Couples relapse prevention sessions after behavioral marital therapy for male alcoholics: Outcomes during the three years after starting treatment. *Journal of Studies on Alcohol, 59(4)*, 357-370.

O'Farrell, T.J. & Fals-Stewart, W. (2000). Behavioral couples therapy for alcoholism and drug abuse. *Journal of Substance Abuse Treatment, 18*, 51-54.

O'Farrell, T.J. & Feehan, M. (1999). Alcoholism treatment and the family: Do family and individual treatments for alcoholic adults have preventive effects for children? *Journal of Studies on Alcohol, Supplement No. 13*, 125-129.

Pinsof, W.M. & Wynne, L.C. (1995). The efficacy of marital and family therapy: An empirical overview, conclusions, and recommendations. *Journal of Marital and Family Therapy, 21(4)*, 585-613.

Prochaska, J.O., DiClemente, C.C. & Norcross, J.C. (1992). In search of how people change. *American Psychologist, 47*, 1102-1114.

Revenstorf, D., Schindler, L. & Hahlweg, K. (1983). Behavioral marital therapy applied in a conjoint and a conjoint-group modality: Short- and long-term effectiveness. *Behavior Therapy, 14*, 614-625.

Roberts, G., Ogborne, A., Leigh, G. & Adam, L. (1999). *Best Practices: Substance Abuse Treatment and Rehabilitation*. Ottawa: Health Canada.

Selekman, M.D. (2002). *Living on the razor's edge: Solution-oriented brief family therapy with self-harming adolescents*. New York: W.W. Norton.

Shadish, W.R., Montgomery, L.M., Wilson, P., Wilson, M.R., Bright, I. & Okwumabua, T. (1993). Effect of family and marital psychotherapies: A meta-analysis. *Journal of Consulting and Clinical Psychology, 61(6),* 992-1002.

Skinner, B.F. (1953). *Science and Human Behavior.* New York: Macmillan.

Spanier, G.B. (1976). Measuring dyadic adjustment: New scales for assessing the quality of marriage and similar dyads. *Journal of Marriage and the Family, 38,* 15-28.

Spanier, G.B. & Thompson, L. (1982). A confirmatory analysis of the Dyadic Adjustment Scale. *Journal of Marriage and the Family, 44,* 731-738.

Stanton, M.D. & Heath, W.H. (1997). Family and marital therapy. In J.H. Lowinson, P. Ruiz, R.B. Millman & J.G. Ingrod (Eds.), *Substance Abuse: A Comprehensive Textbook* (3rd ed., pp. 448-454). Baltimore: Williams & Wilkins.

Stanton, M.D. & Shadish, W.R. (1997). Outcome, attrition, and family-couples treatment for drug abuse: A meta-analysis and review of the controlled, comparative studies. *Psychological Bulletin, 122(2),* 170-191.

Wilson, G.L., Bornstein, P.H. & Wilson, L.J. (1988). Treatment of relationship dysfunction: An empirical evaluation of group and conjoint behavioral marital therapy. *Journal of Consulting and Clinical Psychology, 56(6),* 929-931.

Zweben, A., Pearlman, S. & Li, S. (1988). A comparison of brief advice and conjoint therapy in the treatment of alcohol abuse: The results of the Marital System study. *British Journal of Addiction, 83,* 899-916.

THE BACKGROUND OF
THE INTEGRATIVE MODEL

The Integrative Model of treatment utilized in the Family Service at the Centre for Addiction and Mental Health (CAMH) incorporates three evidenced-based approaches that have been established as effective with a wide variety of populations and problems: family systems theory and family therapy, solution-focused therapy and cognitive behavioural therapy. Family systems theory is the overarching paradigm that informs the conceptual framework of the Integrative Model, while cognitive behavioural and solution-focused approaches make up most of the core interventions utilized in this model. An overview of each of these approaches follows to highlight the backdrop of the Integrative Model.

FAMILY SYSTEMS THEORY

Family therapy and family systems theory evolved from diverse avenues of inquiry and practice, including social scientists' interest in group dynamics of the early 1920s; the child guidance movement of the 1940s and 1950s; the experience of a large number of social workers engaged in front-line work with troubled families during this same period; the development of marriage-counselling centres; and research into the relationship between family dynamics and schizophrenia (Nichols & Schwartz, 1998). Of the latter, the Palo Alto group (Gregory Bateson, Jay Haley, John Weakland) made a significant contribution to family systems theory and family therapy, despite the fact that their perspective on family functioning with relation to mental illness was different from the way that most practitioners would perceive it today. (See Nichols & Schwartz (2001): Chapter 2, "The Evolution of Family Therapy.") Bateson was interested in cybernetics, anthropology and communications theory, and he brought concepts — such as "report" and "command" functions of a communicated message and the "double bind" message — from these areas into the emerging field of family therapy.

Cybernetics theory played a significant role as a founding principle of family systems theory. In North America, prior to the middle of the 20th century, the family was not seen as a useful or legitimate focus of clinical attention, but rather as a collection of individuals; and it was the individuals themselves whose characteristics were of concern to researchers and clinicians (McCollum & Trepper, 2001). Cybernetics, developed by mathematician Norbert Weiner at MIT (Nichols & Schwartz, 1998), described the workings of self-correcting systems. The core concept in cybernetics is the "feedback loop," which is the process whereby information is fed back to the system in order to maintain or alter the workings of the system. Negative feedback among the parts of a system reduces deviation in the whole system, while positive feedback amplifies deviation. One example of cybernetic operation is the way that a thermostat controls the amount of heat produced by a furnace by getting feedback from the environment through its heat sensor.

In adapting cybernetics theory to family functioning, Bateson shifted the notion of causality with respect to family problems from linear to circular causality. Instead of viewing family problems as the (linear) result of past events, Bateson described the cause of family problems as part of ongoing, circular feedback loops (McCollum &

Trepper, 2001). Bateson and his Palo Alto group infused the notion of the system into family theory, generating a picture of the family system as one in which the whole cannot be understood except through the relationship between its parts. In his view, families include multiple sets of systems, and these systems interact continuously, providing feedback that maintains or alters the system as a whole. When drugs and alcohol are considered from the perspective of a systems approach, the behaviour of the person with the substance use problem affects individual family members in multiple ways and the reactions of family members affect the experiences and the actions of the person who is using drugs or alcohol. This pattern occurs within the family of origin and across extended systems as well.

FAMILY THERAPY

Family therapy encompasses several approaches to family functioning and therapy. Included in these approaches to family therapy are the following: intergenerational, structural, strategic, experiential and communications, feminist, social learning, cognitive behavioural and psychoanalytic. What all of the family therapy approaches have in common is the conceptualization of the family as a system, and a focus of clinical attention on the relationships between people to a greater extent than on intrapsychic phenomena and individual behaviour. From within this paradigm, the Integrative Model draws primarily, but not solely, upon principles and techniques from intergenerational, structural and strategic family therapies.

Intergenerational family therapy was conceived by Murray Bowen, who was one of the most influential pioneers of the family therapy movement, and his theory of family functioning was the most comprehensive within the family systems paradigm (Nichols & Schwartz, 1998). Bowen (1978) argued that family members' problems were related to poor "differentiation of self," which refers to a person's ability to separate his or her emotional functioning from his or her intellectual functioning, and he further postulated a "multigenerational transmission process" whereby lower levels of differentiation get transmitted from one generation to the next. Intergenerational family therapy, therefore, focuses on processes among generations. The Family Genogram (or Family Tree) is a technique that is often used to explore these processes.

Structural family therapy grew out of the clinical work of Salvador Minuchin (1974). Minuchin's perspective on family functioning and therapy was informed by his work with underprivileged families and institutionalized children (Nichols & Schwartz, 1998). Minuchin proposed that problems were the result of dysfunctional structures within the family. Thus, the goals of structural family therapy are to clarify boundaries, subsystems and power hierarchies within the family (as well as the external social forces that impinge upon the family) and to reorganize the family into a more functional structure. These goals are accomplished first by "joining" with the family from a position of acceptance and respectful leadership, and then restructuring the family by utilizing techniques such as "enactment," in which family members are asked to role-play their relationship patterns, and "reframing," or changing the labels attached to behaviours from the perspective of understanding the family structure.

Strategic family therapy is a brief, problem-focused therapy that was developed by Jay Haley, who had worked with Salvador Minuchin, and Cloe Madanes, at the Philadelphia Child Guidance Clinic. In 1974, Madanes and Haley opened the Family Therapy Institute in Washington, D.C. (Nichols & Schwartz, 1998). Their brand of family systems theory, which continues to be widely used, sees family interactions as communication patterns. Haley (1976) described the notion of the "behavioural sequence." Behavioural sequences are the occurrences of problems in families, viewed in terms of regular, predictable patterns of family interactions or events. Haley suggested that if you change a step along the sequence of events, then you will often change the outcome. In order to effect these changes, strategic family therapists make use of a wide variety of creative techniques (Nichols & Schwartz, 1998; McCollum & Trepper, 2001), including "reframing" interventions to alter family members' perceptions of the problem and "paradoxical interventions," which utilize client resistance in the service of eliciting positive behaviour change by encouraging its opposite.

As mentioned above, there are a number of other family therapy approaches that are reflected to a lesser extent in the CAMH Integrated Model. Carl Whitaker is the primary proponent of experiential family therapy, a somewhat atheoretical, spontaneous approach to family therapy, while Virginia Satir's approach, which has also been described as experiential, is known as a communications therapy. Satir used creative techniques such as "family sculpting" (role plays) to help family members become aware of their familial roles and interrelationships (McCollum & Trepper, 2001). Social learning and cognitive behavioural approaches to family therapy focus on the identification of skill deficits, behaviour modification and positive reinforcement strategies, skill-building techniques, and specific behavioural goals, such as problem solving and contingency contracting (Nichols & Schwartz, 1998; McCollum & Trepper, 2001). Many of the pioneers of the family systems approach were trained as psychoanalysts, including Nathan Akerman, Ian Alger, Murray Bowen, Lyman Wynne, Theodore Lidz, Israel Zwerling, Ivan Boszormenyi-Nagy, Carl Whitaker, Don Jackson and Salvador Minuchin (Nichols & Schwartz, 1998). There are a number of different schools of psychoanalytic theory, including object relations theory, self psychology and Freudian theory. Overall, within the psychoanalytic framework, behaviour is the result of intrapsychic factors to a greater extent than external factors, and the goal of therapy is to free family members from the unconscious forces that limit healthy functioning (Nichols & Schwartz, 1998).

Feminist family therapy adds a different perspective to the other approaches by utilizing a feminist framework to deconstruct the gender biases and power hierarchies inherent in the more traditional approaches, and to recognize the realities of women's experiences. Proponents of the feminist family therapy perspective are Marianne Walters, Betty Carter, Monica McGoldrick, Peggy Papp and Olga Silverstein (McCollum & Trepper, 2001; Nichols & Schwartz, 1998).

SOLUTION-FOCUSED THERAPY

Solution-focused therapy grew out of the other family systems approaches, primarily from strategic family therapy. (See Nichols & Schwartz (Chapter 11; 1998) for a detailed discussion of the historical line tracing the development of solution-focused therapy from its roots in strategic family therapy.) The major figures spearheading this approach are Insoo Kim Berg and Steve de Shazer, who were trained as brief therapists following the strategic approach of Jay Haley and Cloe Madanes. The theoretical perspective underlying solution-focused therapy is somewhat sparse, because the focus is on generating solutions to problems rather than considering how these problems arose (Nichols & Schwartz, 1998).

Solution-focused therapy is a brief therapy treatment that is technique-driven and future-oriented. While problems are the source of therapeutic material, building and maintaining solutions to these problems are the focus of therapy. Assessing motivation is an important aspect of solution-focused therapy. A method for assessing motivation is to determine whether or not the client is one of the following: a "customer," who recognizes that there is a problem and wants help to try and solve it; a "complainant," who sees that a problem exists and wants the therapist to make someone else solve it; or a "visitor," who denies that a problem exists and does not want the therapist's help (Berg & Miller, 1992).

Recently, solution-focused therapists have turned their attention to problem substance use (Berg & Miller, 1992; McCollum & Trepper, 2001; Selekman, 2002). As in solution-focused therapy for other problems and issues, solution-focused therapists working with families of substance users focus on solutions rather than problems; join empathically with family members; negotiate a contract; help clients create measurable goals; help clients develop a vision; track problem-solution sequences; and seek and enlarge successes (McCollum & Trepper, 2001).

Solution-focused therapists maintain a focus on positive elements of client behaviours. Some of the techniques used in this therapy include searching out underlying congruent meanings behind opposing goals and positions; using the Miracle Question to develop a positive vision; scaling; tracking problem and solution sequences; listening for exceptions to the problem and calling attention to them; and complimenting successes.

COGNITIVE BEHAVIOURAL THERAPY (CBT)

Cognitive behavioural therapy (CBT) is a blend of cognitive therapy and behaviour therapy. Cognitive therapy, pioneered by Aaron Beck (1921-) and Albert Ellis (1929-), asserts that change in behaviours and emotions occurs through change in thinking (cognitions); behaviour therapy is based on principles of operant conditioning (Skinner, 1953) and learning theory (Bandura & Walters, 1963). According to social learning theory, human behaviour is learned, as opposed to being the result of innate drives, and it is governed by eliciting factors. From the tenets of operant conditioning, we know that behaviour is affected by its consequences, that reinforcements affect the rate of target behaviours, and that contingencies define the relationship between a behaviour and its consequences. The addition of the cognitive approach to behaviour theory meant an increasing emphasis on cognitions and the recognition of the need for attitude change to promote and maintain behaviour change. The efficacy and effectiveness of CBT for depression and anxiety has been borne out in an extensive body of research (Antony & Swinson, 1996; Beck, 1976; Dobson, 1989).

Cognitive behavioural therapy tends to be relatively short term. The focus of the therapy is on internal and external behaviours as opposed to explanations for behaviour, and it is problem-oriented (as opposed to insight-oriented or experiential). Therefore symptoms, such as panic attacks, depressive ideation and alcohol or drug use, are the legitimate focus of clinical attention. The goals of therapy include restructuring of faulty thoughts, perceptions and beliefs, and developing positive coping skills in order to foster emotional and behavioural change. CBT interventions include challenging irrational beliefs, psychoeducation, communication and social skills-building exercises, and homework assignments.